D0419045

Fiction
at this level

FISHING FOR
TROUBLE
DAVID AND HELEN ORME

978 1 4451 1812 3 pb

FOOTBALL
LEGEND
DAVID AND HELEN ORME

978 1 4451 1811 6 pb

VAMPIRES ARE
SO BORING
DAVID AND HELEN ORME

978 1 4451 1813 0 pb

MY NAME IS
COLEN
STEVE BARLOW AND STEVE SKIDMORE

978 1 4451 3070 5 pb

**DEVIL'S
TEETH**
STEVE BARLOW AND STEVE SKIDMORE

978 1 4451 3054 5 pb

**SPACE
STATION ALERT**
DAVID AND HELEN ORME

978 1 4451 3068 2 pb

Graphic fiction
at this level

DEMON
STREAK
JONNY ZUCKER AND STEVE SAMPSON

978 1 4451 1799 7 pb

**FULL METAL
HERO**
JONNY ZUCKER AND DAN BOULTWOOD

978 1 4451 1801 7 pb

**TERROR
BEAST**
JONNY ZUCKER AND MACK CHATER

978 1 4451 1800 0 pb

**ALIEN
ACADEMY**
JONNY ZUCKER AND SEAN PENTNEY

978 1 4451 3088 0 pb

**DOWNHILL
RACERS**
JONNY ZUCKER AND SEAN BUCHANAN

978 1 4451 3089 7 pb

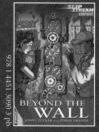

BEYOND THE
WALL
JONNY ZUCKER AND TOMAS ARANDA

978 1 4451 3090 3 pb

Non-fiction
at this level

BIZARRE
BUILDINGS
ANNE ROONEY

978 1 4451 1952 6 hb
978 1 4451 3229 7 pb

CRAZY
FOOD
ANNE ROONEY

978 1 4451 1954 0 hb
978 1 4451 3228 0 pb

WACKY
SPORTS
ANNE ROONEY

978 1 4451 1953 3 hb
978 1 4451 3227 3 pb

AMAZING
PETS
ANNE ROONEY

978 1 4451 3050 7 hb

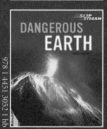

DANGEROUS
EARTH
ANNE ROONEY

978 1 4451 3052 1 hb

WORLD'S
TOUGHEST
ANNE ROONEY

978 1 4451 3035 4 hb

SLIP STREAM

DANGEROUS EARTH

ANNE ROONEY

EDGE
FRANKLIN
WATTS

LONDON·SYDNEY

First published in 2014 by
Franklin Watts
338 Euston Road
London NW1 3BH

Franklin Watts Australia
Level 17/207 Kent Street
Sydney NSW 2000

© Franklin Watts 2014

(hb) ISBN: 978 1 4451 3052 1
(Library ebook) ISBN: 978 1 4451 3053 8

Dewey classification number: 551

All rights reserved

The right of Anne Rooney to be
identified as the author of this Work
has been asserted in accordance
with the Copyright, Designs and
Patents Act, 1988.

A CIP catalogue record for this book
is available from the British Library.

Series Editors: Adrian Cole and Jackie Hamley
Series Advisors: Diana Bentley and Dee Reid
Series Designer: Peter Scoulding
Designer: Cathryn Gilbert
Picture Researcher: Diana Morris

Printed in China

Franklin Watts is a division of
Hachette Children's Books,
an Hachette UK company.
www.hachette.co.uk

Acknowledgements:
All Action/Empics/PAI: 8.
Jack Ammit/Shutterstock: front cover.
Antara/AP/Empics/PAI: 23t.
AP/PAI: 15, 16.
Bluesand Views/istockphoto: 7.
Central Press/Getty Images: 22c.
Jim Edds/Corbis: 4cr, 19.
Kevin Frayer/AP/PAI: 9.
Owen Humphreys/PA/PIA: 20.
Harley McCabe /istockphoto: 4-5b, 6b, 10b,
17b, 18b, 22b.
Roland Nagy/Dreamstime: 23b.
NASA: 1, 18c.
Douglas Peebles/Alamy: 4cl, 11.
Proioxis/istockphoto: 6.
Martin Rietze/Westend61GMbh/Alamy: 12.
Richard Roscoe/StocktrekImages/Alamy: 13.
Slim Sepp/Dreamstime: 10c.
Mainichi Shimbun/Reuters: 5c, 14.
Yomiuri Shimbun/AFP/Getty Images: 17c.
Denis TangneyJr/istockphoto: 21.

Every attempt has been made to
clear copyright. Should there be any
inadvertent omission, please apply
to the publisher for rectification.

ABERDEENSHIRE LIBRARIES	
3144613	
Bertrams	25/07/2014
J551	£8.99

CONTENTS

LIVING WITH DANGER

Earth is a dangerous place.

Natural events kill thousands of people around the world every year. Volcanoes shoot molten rock, strong winds strike and floods wash people away.

SHAKING GROUND

The land and sea are on large slabs of rock.
They move very, very slowly.

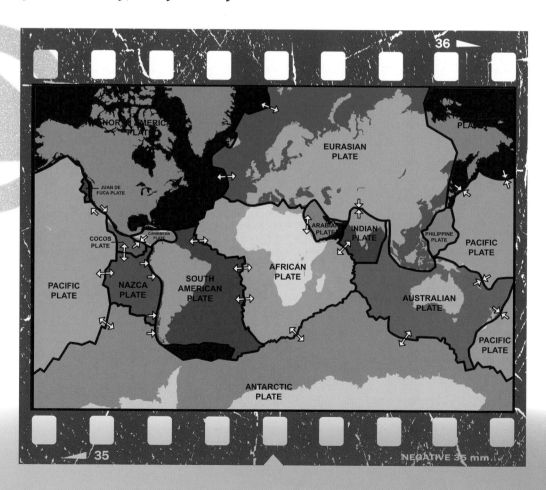

Sometimes they get stuck or push together. Then they jolt and make an earthquake.

An earthquake shakes the ground. Buildings fall down, and roads and bridges break apart.

Rescuers use dogs and machines to help find people who are trapped.

FIRE AND ROCK

A volcano forms when red-hot molten rock breaks through the Earth's surface.

Volcanoes shoot the molten rock, called lava, into the air.

Hot winds and ash clouds rush over the land.
They destroy everything in their path.

SEA FLOOD

A tsunami (say 'soon-army') is a powerful wave.
The tsunami rushes across the sea and crashes
onto the land.

The tsunami destroys roads and buildings.

It washes people away.
When the water flows away
the land is left in ruins.

SPIRAL STORM

A hurricane is a very strong storm.

Its strong winds can destroy
buildings and kill people.

WEATHER WARNING

Extreme weather can cause death and destruction. Floods are caused by heavy rain.

Heat waves are caused by hot sun. Heavy snowfalls are caused by blizzards.

WORLD'S WORST

Earthquake: China, 1556.

Flood: China, 1931.

Volcano: Indonesia, 1815.

Hurricane: Bangladesh, 1970.

NEGATIVE 35 mm

Tsunami: Indian Ocean, 2004.

Heat wave: Europe, 2003.

INDEX

FOR TEACHERS

About SLIPSTREAM

Slipstream is a series of expertly levelled books designed for pupils who are struggling with reading. Its unique three-strand approach through fiction, graphic fiction and non-fiction gives pupils a rich reading experience that will accelerate their progress and close the reading gap.

At the heart of every Slipstream non-fiction book is exciting information. Easily accessible words and phrases ensure that pupils both decode and comprehend, and the topics really engage older struggling readers.

Whether you're using Slipstream Level 2 for Guided Reading or as an independent read, here are some suggestions:

1. Make each reading session successful. Talk about the text before the pupil starts reading. Introduce any unfamiliar vocabulary.

2. Encourage the pupil to talk about the book using a range of open questions. For example, which natural events have they experienced?

3. Discuss the differences between reading non-fiction, fiction and graphic fiction. Which do they prefer?

For guidance, SLIPSTREAM Level 2 – Dangerous Earth has been approximately measured to:

National Curriculum Level: 2b
Reading Age: 7.6–8.0
Book Band: Purple

ATOS: 2.4 *
Guided Reading Level: I
Lexile® Measure (confirmed): 600L

*Please check actual Accelerated Reader™ book level and quiz availability at www.arbookfind.co.uk